SALISBURY to EXETER CENTRAL

ISBN 978 0-9553334-1-5

British Library Cataloguing Data: a Catalogue for this book is available from the British Library
© Derek Phillips 2007
Graphics & Design by Flaydemouse, 8 Buckland Road Yeovil, Somerset BA21 5EA
Printed by J.H.Haynes & Co, Sparkford, England
First Published in 2007 by Footplate Publishing, 4 White Mead, Yeovil, Somerset BA21 3RX

Front cover; Rebuild No. 35007 *Aberdeen Commonwealth* at Salisbury with a train for Exeter.
The late P.M.Alexander/Colour-Rail BRS1130

Rear cover; The same locomotive as seen on the front jacket No.35007 *Aberdeen Commonwealth* here in blue livery and air smooth casing at Exeter Central on 6 June 1950.
The late P.K.Tunks courtesy A.B.Jeffrey/Colour-Rail BRS227

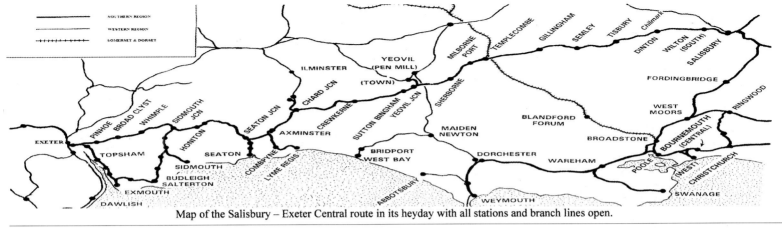

Map of the Salisbury – Exeter Central route in its heyday with all stations and branch lines open.

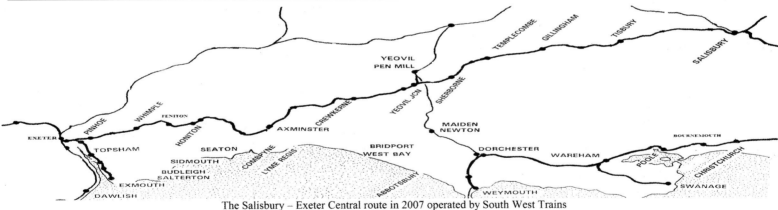

The Salisbury – Exeter Central route in 2007 operated by South West Trains

Contents

Introduction

Unbelievably (how time flies) 2007 is the fortieth Anniversary of the ending of main line steam on the Southern Region of the then nationalised railway industry of the United Kingdom.

I have known the route between Salisbury and Exeter Central since I was a boy and well remember seeing for the first time one of the superb Pacific Locomotives designed by Oliver Vaughan Bulleid arriving at Yeovil Junction during the late 1940s complete with air smooth casing and piercing electric head lamps.

Memories abound of watching the *Atlantic Coast Express* and *Devon Belle* running through Yeovil Junction non-stop. Unfortunately those days have gone forever, only memories remain.

Of course our trip to Yeovil Junction was via the branch train from Yeovil Town Station this in itself was an adventure, as we were only travelling to the Junction station and back to see off my Grandmother who would be travelling to London for a visit to relatives. In those days of course, no computers, television or family cars, so an occasional trip on the little branch train was worthwhile.

Many years later as a young fireman based at the locomotive depot at Yeovil Town I worked on all classes of steam locomotives during the 1950s and 60s including of course coming to grips with the superb Bulleid Pacific's which were extremely free-steaming locomotives, although as a fireman I preferred the locomotives in their original air smoothed form to the Rebuilds.

And like my footplate comrades from the locomotive sheds at Yeovil Town, Exmouth Junction and Salisbury I have had my share of good and bad trips on locomotives at all hours of the day and night in weather conditions fair or foul on the gradients of the Southern route to the West.

The photographs contained within the pages of this book, only give a glimpse of the steam power that was once a daily feature of the main railway route between Salisbury and Exeter Central.

I would like to thank Eric Youldon for rechecking my texts and advising me on various technical points. Mike King, South West Circle, Transport Treasury, Southern Images, Roger Carpenter, H.M.R.S, Paul Chancellor, Ron White Colour-Rail.

Derek Phillips
Yeovil
Somerset

Class 5MT 4-6-0 No. 73117 *Vivien* arrives at Salisbury in August 1964 with a cross-country Portsmouth to South Wales passenger train. As a fireman I preferred the Class 5 Standards to the smaller Class 4MT 2-6-0 Class.

Coal is being shovelled forward, the tender refilled and the driver of No. 35022 *Holland America Line* wanders around the front end of the locomotive for a last minute spot of oiling, before departing for Waterloo with the Atlantic Coast Express from Salisbury. I well remember as a young engine cleaner, being sent on loan from Yeovil Town shed to Salisbury and spent my first summer on the railway shovelling coal forward and watering the locomotives working through from Exeter to Waterloo. Only six minutes were allowed for crew changeover and coal shovelling etc. The footbridge, now removed, once connected with the GWR station.

G.Heiron/Transport Treasury

Left:
Atmospheric night shot at Salisbury as the fierce glow from the firebox reflects inside the cab of No. 35010 *Blue Star* on a freight train. The lighting also emphasises the steam escaping from the safety valves, upraised signal arm and the goods yard lamps in the distance.

G.Heiron/Transport Treasury

Battle of Britain Class No.34058 *Sir Frederick Pile* leaves Salisbury heading for Waterloo with a passenger train. Bulleid Light Pacifics from 34001-70 had 8ft 6in wide cabs. 34071 onwards had the 9ft wide cabs. It was only when any of the 34001-70 series were rebuilt that the cabs were widened to 9ft. The air smooth casing was removed when rebuilding occurred in 1960. The locomotive was withdrawn in 1964. The reporting number is on the top bracket and the Nine Elms roster number on the lower disc

G.Heiron/Transport Treasury

Right:
The Pride of Salisbury Shed No.30453 *King Arthur* complete with the early BR lion & wheel totem on the tender, pulls away from Salisbury and heads for Waterloo with a passenger train in June 1950. The locomotive has the Drummond watercart tender usual with the 448-57 batch of Arthurs until the mid to late 1950s.

J.C.Flemons/Transport Treasury

T9 4-4-0 No.305 was converted to oil burning in January 1947 the 1,600 gallon oil tank can be seen perched in the coal space on the tender, electric lighting powered by a Stone's steam generator was installed in February 1948. A total of fifteen T9 locomotives were converted to oil burning and electric lights. No.305 seen here at Salisbury on 11 September 1948 has just uncoupled from a Portsmouth-Cardiff service and the crew pose for the camera whilst setting off to the locomotive shed.

A.E.West.

Left:
Class L12 No. 30421 still in Southern livery trundles through the West End of Salisbury station with a freight train in June 1950. This actual locomotive whilst hauling an up Plymouth Boat train came to grief at the east end of the station in 1906. The story of that dreadful accident and the loss of life incurred (29 in total including the Driver and Fireman of No. 421) has been well recorded elsewhere, suffice to say. But the locomotive was relatively undamaged and although allocated to Salisbury was diplomatically moved to Bournemouth after repair at Nine Elms. The locomotive dating from October 1904 was withdrawn in August 1951.

J.C.Flemons/Transport Treasury

In Southern Railway livery with a BR number on the cabside No.35017 *Belgian Marine* hustles the prestige all Pullman Devon Belle through Salisbury to the engine changeover special stop at Wilton on 11 September 1948. The Devon Belle had began running a year previously on 20 June.

A.E.West

Right

No. 4084 *Aberystwyth Castle* with express headlamp code - departs from Salisbury and heads towards Westbury with a Portsmouth-Cardiff cross country service in June 1950.

J.C.Flemons/Transport Treasury

Activity at the West End of Salisbury station as No.6935 *Browsholme Hall* departs for Westbury with a cross-country service in June 1950. S15 4-6-0 No.30826 with tail lamp on the buffer beam is fresh off shed, and has coupled up to a train for the Exeter line. No.30450 *Sir Kay* stands in the yard on the right.

J.C.Flemons/Transport Treasury

Rebuilt West Country Class 4-6-0 No.34013 *Okehampton* stands in the down bay at Salisbury with the 3.05pm to Exeter Central. As the engine is fresh off shed, the fire will be burning through rapidly, the fireman will have let the boiler level drop, and can then put the injector on in order to keep her quiet whilst standing in the station.

Alec Swain/Transport Treasury

Fresh off shed No.21C15 *Rotterdam Lloyd* in Southern Railway livery trundles towards Salisbury station to work a Waterloo service on 11 September 1948, the GWR locomotive shed can be seen in the background.

A.E.West

Arriving from the West 34044 *Woolacombe* and an unidentified 4-6-0 arrive at Salisbury in June 1950. As a fireman I would have the fire banked up, boiler filled and the footplate all clean and tidy in readiness for our relief crew who would be waiting for us at the far end of the platform, it was a matter of pride to hand a locomotive over in the best condition possible.

J.C.Flemons/Transport

Salisbury June 1950 and No.35017 *Belgian Marine* powers the down Atlantic Coast Express towards the first advertised stop at Sidmouth Junction. Note the footplatemen on the right walking back to the locomotive shed. I have done this myself many times, although a bit dodgy with locomotives moving in and out of the shed.

J.C.Flemons/Transport Treasury

S15 Class 4-6-0 30838 has char being shovelled from the smokebox on the disposal pit at Salisbury shed on 18 April 1964. The box on the running plate above the rear coupled wheels housed the battery for the Automatic Warning System which in the case of 30838 was fitted in April 1960.I have seen this pit absolutely full of locomotives awaiting disposal, each one moving down in turn after attention to fire, smokebox and ashpan, and after refilling with coal and water, the shed turners would move the relevant locomotive on to the turntable, and thence to its correct place in the shed for its next duty.

Alec Swain/Transport Treasury

Drummond M7 0-4-4T No.30673 seen here in superb external condition on Salisbury shed on 16 June 1957 was a long time Salisbury station shunter. I liked working on this type of locomotive, we had the push & pull fitted versions 30129 and 30131 at Yeovil Town shed for working the connecting service between Yeovil Town and Yeovil Junction stations.

Alec Swain/Transport Treasury

Standard Class 5MT 4-6-0 No.73117 *Vivien* awaits a return to its home shed of 70A (Nine Elms) on 18 April 1964. Salisbury was a splendid shed, the Driver's cabin was full of cigarette and pipe smoke, the kettle always on the boil as crews from various sheds trooped in and out again, footplatemen's cabins were always a hotbed of debate and gossip.

Alec Swain/Transport Treasury

The fire has been made ready, and the safety valves lift as Rebuild No.34009 *Lyme Regis* stands on Salisbury shed on 18 April 1964.
Alec Swain/Transport Treasury

The starting signal is raised as No.34076 *41 Squadron* departs from Gillingham with the 15.05 Salisbury – Exeter Central on 5 September 1964. If a crew were short of steam with an Exeter bound train on the ascent from Tisbury to Semley the run downhill with regulator closed to Gillingham would usually bring the steam gauge around to full pressure.

SOUTHERN-Images (www.southern-images.co.uk)

The tall chimney of the local brickworks looms in the background as Standard Class 4MT 2-6-0 No.76007 arrives at Gillingham with the 15.50 Yeovil Town - Salisbury on 5 September 1964. In common with other fireman I always had the fire of my locomotive built right up here with a train for Salisbury as the formidable four mile long Semley bank with gradients of 1 in 130 and 1 in 100 starts at the end of the up platform.

SOUTHERN-Images (www.southern-images.co.uk)

35018 *British India Line* sweeps into Templecombe with a down service from Waterloo.

W.V. Mace Collection/Mile Post 92¹/₂

Right:

Maunsell U Class 2-6-0 No.31791 stands alongside the up platform at Templecombe on 20 April 1948. The front end of the locomotive has the unusual combination of disc codes and a headlamp. In my view this suggests that when the loco arrived at Yeovil Junction tender first from Yeovil Town shed in light engine mode (complete with tail lamp) the fireman forgot to remove the lamp before coupling up to the coaches for this train.

A.E. West

On the S & D side of Templecombe station Class Z 0-8-0T No. 30953 stands attached to the rear of the 11.45am to Bournemouth in readiness to pilot the train down the short distance to the S & D main line, the train engine (at the far end of the train) will then be facing the correct way and continue its journey on 26 April 1955.

H.M.R.S ACD901

Left:
S15 4-6-0 No. 830 in Southern Railway livery is standing at the rear of an up train at Templecombe on 23 July 1948, as coaches were attached and detached from main line trains here daily, this view would suggest that something of the kind is happening here.

A.E.West

Maid of all work – 0-6-0T No.47542 stands alongside the S & D platform at Templecombe on 29 August 1961. The S.R. main line up platform is also occupied as a coach can be glimpsed to the left of the locomotive.

A.E.West

The Somerset & Dorset locomotive shed as viewed from the elevated spur line to the upper station on 19 July 1948. An abundance of loaded coal trucks stands in the siding, the S.R. West of England main line can be seen on the horizon and the S & D main line lies in the foreground.

H.M.R.S ACE428

Templecombe upper yard shunting locomotive remained under the control of Yeovil Town Locomotive Depot until June 1950 when G6 0-6-0 No.30274 seen here in the upper yard on 13 March 1952 was transferred to the S&D shed. This locomotive being replaced by Z Class No. 30953 in December 1954.

A.E.West

Right:

The Templecombe starting signal is raised for the Driver of No.35019 *French Line C.G.T.* (in blue livery) as he awaits the 'right away' from the guard with a train for Exeter Central on 27 March 1950.The fireman is in the tender dragging some decent coal forward with the coal pick, a task I have done many times myself, especially at a station stop, nip up and get some good lumpy coal forward. The upper yard, which was always busy with transfer freight traffic between the S&D and the Southern Region, can be seen to the right.

A.E.West

The fireman of 30847 (72B) throws coal forward on the tender in preparation for working the 15.34 Templecombe – Exeter Central on 1 May 1953. The locomotive and three-coach set are standing in the down sidings at Templecombe. I have worked this turn as a fireman many times. After the departure of a down semi-fast we would reverse into the station and pick up passengers for our train.

A.E.West

Battle of Britain Class No. 34076 *41 Squadron* near Templecombe with the 11.52am Yeovil Town – Salisbury on 5 September 1964. The fireman will have the injector turned on topping the boiler up for the descent into the station.

N15 Class No. 792 Sir *Hervis de Revel* arrives alongside the crowded up platform at Yeovil Junction with a Sunday Plymouth to Brighton service in 1938.

SOUTHERN-Images (www.southern-images.co.uk)

Left:

The Driver of No. 73085 *Melisande* after tackling the ascent from Sherborne is cracking on through Milborne Port with the 11.am Padstow – Waterloo the last up Atlantic Coast Express on 5 September 1964. This was the third portion of the up ACE to run on the final day, being preceded by No.35009 *Shaw Savill* with the first (Ilfracombe) portion, followed by the Torrington portion hauled by 34093 *Saunton*.

SOUTHERN Images (www.southern-images.co.uk)

With steam escaping from the safety valves, and a hint of smoke from the chimney of No.30798 *Sir Hectimere* the fireman has his fire all ready in preparation for the journey ahead whilst standing in the up yard at Yeovil Junction on 29 September 1961.

A.E.West

left:
Class 4MT 2-6-0 No.76066 runs alongside the up platform at Yeovil Junction with a pick-up freight from Chard Junction. The lack of a disc code on the front of the locomotive seems to suggest that the fireman, after travelling tender-first to Crewkerne and Chard Junction has forgotten to remove the discs from the rear of the locomotive for the return journey. I know because I have done it myself on this particular diagram worked by Yeovil Town footplatemen.

Paul Chancellor Collection

Rebuild West Country Pacific No.34100 *Appledore* lifts her safety valves impatiently at Yeovil Junction before departing for Exeter Central with Set 533.

Paul Chancellor Collection

M7 0-4-4T No. 30131 leaves Yeovil Junction hauling Set No.373 on the short run to Yeovil Town station on 22 August 1959. I liked our M7s and have fond memories of 30129 and 30131. A train is also signalled on the up through line.

A.E.West

The 'boards' on the superb six arm gantry at Yeovil Junction are against N15 4-6-0 No.746 *Pendragon* whilst standing at the up platform on 11 September 1948.

A.E.West

Right:
Rebuild Merchant Navy Class No.35022 *Holland America Line* takes water at Yeovil Junction whilst en route from Waterloo to Seaton Junction with the L.C.G.B. East Devon Rail Tour on 28 February 1965.

Alex Swain/Transport Treasury

Merchant Navy Class 4-6-2 No. 35006 *Peninsular & Oriental Steam Navigation Co.* bowls along near Crewkerne with a three coach Set on 26 March 1950.

A.E.West

Right:
No. 30827 arrives at Crewkerne with an up stopping train on 26 July 1958, a down train is also signalled as the Crewkerne down starter and Crewkerne Gates distant signals can be seen in the off position over the bridge.

R.C.Riley/Transport Treasury

Merchant Navy Class No.35004 *Cunard White Star* is seen here cracking on with the down Devon Belle on 15 May 1948 on the 1 in 80 approach to Crewkerne Tunnel. One of our S15 4-6-0s would be almost a walking pace at this spot whilst slogging up the grade with a heavy Exeter bound freight train.

A.E.West

Left:
S15 4-6-0 No.30844 (72A) arrives with an up freight at Crewkerne on 30 March 1954. Considerable shunting was done here, main exports being Calves transported in horse boxes to Maude, Scotland, sugar beet, coal, timber and agricultural products

A.E.West

Left:

The Devon Belle was one of those rare trains where the rear was as much photographed as the locomotive on the front. The Pullman Observation Car seen here on the rear of the up train approaching Crewkerne Tunnel on 15 May 1948 being one of two such vehicles converted from existing Pullman Cars, weighing 33 tons each car comprised a bar, pantry, lavatory and an observation saloon which had seating for 27 passengers in single and double tub seats.

A.E.West

N15 4-6-0 No. 30744 *Maid of Astolat* runs out of the 206 yard long Crewkerne Tunnel with a passenger train 16 April 1949.

A.E.West

A rare visitor to the South Western main line 9F 2-10-0 No. 92205 hauling an up ballast train, awaits the home signal to clear at Chard Junction on 2 February 1962.

A.E. West

Left:
Chard Junction 2 February 1962 an up special to Waterloo hauled by Rebuilt Battle of Britain class No.34059 *Sir Archibald Sinclair*. The train is formed of Cafeteria Car 7954 next to the locomotive followed by three open saloons and a brake composite.

A.E. West

S15 4-6-0 No.30832 with a train for Exeter Central at Axminster on 21 June 1951. A pair of footplatemen can be seen by the water column to the right of the locomotive.

H.M.R.S.AES812

Adams 0415 Radial 4-4-2T No.30582 stands alongside the branch platform at Axminster on 23 July 1958 with the 12.33 to Lyme Regis.

H.M.R.S ABJ719

Rebuild No. 34056 *Croydon* stands alongside the up platform at Axminster with a passenger train for Waterloo.

SOUTHERN-Images (www.southern-images.co.uk)

Left:
The crew of Class U 2-6-0 No. 31610 refill the locomotive tender with water at Axminster on 14 May 1959. The fireman reposes on the tender, whilst the Driver rolls his cigarette.

A.E.West

The Driver of N15 No.457 *Sir Bedivere* looks pensively at the photographer whilst awaiting the right away with an Exeter train at Seaton Junction on 16 September 1948. The superb LSWR lower quadrant starter and advanced starter signals are off giving a clear road ahead. From here is the ascent on the fearsome Honiton Incline an eight-mile climb mostly at 1 in 80 to the tunnel at the summit. Like all firemen I had to have the fire just right here.

A.E.West

Left:
No.35022 *Holland America Line* hauling the East Devon Rail Tour previously seen at Yeovil Junction has now arrived at Axminster on 28 February 1965. Passengers had the option to alight here for a trip to Lyme Regis, which was top & tailed by 41291/41206 whilst the main train with 35022 went ahead to Seaton Junction. Branch lines visited that day included; Seaton, Sidmouth, and Exmouth via Tipton St. Johns and Exmouth to Exeter Central thence return to Waterloo with 35022.

Alec Swain/Transport Treasury

No. 35016 *Elders Fyffes* in blue livery takes the through track and storms through Seaton Junction with the down Atlantic Coast Express at 1.50pm on 12 March 1952.   *A.E.West*

Right Top:
No. 34055 *Fighter Pilot* arrives at Seaton Junction with the 12.58pm Exeter Central to Salisbury on 12 March 1952.

A.E.West

Right Bottom:
With the home signal off for the up through line No.35004 *Cunard White Star* in blue livery runs through Seaton Junction with a freight train from Exmouth Junction on 12 March 1952.   *A.E.West*

Having given members of the L.C.G.B. East Devon Rail Tour a trip along the Axminster-Lyme Regis branch - Nos.41206 & 41291 (seen in the background) have arrived at Seaton Junction and reversed their coaches on to 80041 for the journey along the branch to Seaton. No. 80041 will return to Seaton Junction and take the passengers onwards to Sidmouth Junction. The main rail tour having gone ahead to Sidmouth Junction behind 35022.

Alec Swain/Transport Treasury

With the train consisting mainly of Pullman Cars 35017 *Belgian Marine* hustles the Waterloo to Plymouth Ian Allan/Trains Illustrated 'Westcountryman' Rail Tour through Seaton Junction at 11.45am on 20 September 1958. Note the LSWR lower quadrant signals on the gantry in the foreground.

A.E.West

Bulleid Pacific No. 34034 *Honiton* arrives at the town it was named after with a passenger train for Salisbury on 20 September 1952.

H.M.R.S. AEW415

Drummond M7 0-4-4T No. 30374 with Set 109 at Honiton on a local train to Exeter on 14 May 1959. The coach stock is interesting as the first coach 1087 is in red livery, followed by 6594 in green.

A.E.West

Lord Nelson Class No. 30861 *Lord Anson* has just run past the Sidmouth Junction outer home signal with the Southern Counties Touring Society 'South Western Limited' on 2 September 1962. From here the coaching stock will be taken to Exmouth via Tipton St. Johns by M7s 30024/25.

Prorail UK (Durrant) Transport Treasury.

The SCTS South Western Limited has arrived at Sidmouth Junction on 2 September 1962. The starting signal is raised allowing 30861 *Lord Anson* to proceed to Exmouth Junction for servicing and turning. Meanwhile M7s Nos. 30025/24 have coupled to the rear of the train to haul the special to Exmouth via Tipton St. Johns and onwards to Exeter Central. Out of the branch lines that once connected to the Salisbury-Exeter line, only the Exeter Central-Exmouth line survives. The link between Yeovil Junction and Pen Mill stations remains but is used only for diversions

Alec Swain/Transport Treasury

Class 4MT 2-6-4T No.80039 stands in the goods yard at Sidmouth Junction on 4 May 1964. Of the crew there is no sign, judging by my own footplate days, there must be a brew up of tea somewhere.

A.E.West

Right:
With the disc code showing that the train has come from the Sidmouth branchline Adams 02 0-4-4T No.199 and Drummond M7 0-4-4T No.123 stand alongside the down platform at Sidmouth Junction c1947 with a local train to Exeter Central.

H.M.R.S AEV624

Exmouth Junction seen here on 23 July 1958 was one of the largest Southern Region Locomotive depots (as was Eastleigh) outside of the London area. A staff of 400 included 120 pairs of Drivers and firemen. I always liked working here, the drivers cabin as always was a hotbed of gossip and arguments, and in contrast to Salisbury the accents were Devon and Cornish except when we Somerset men from Yeovil were there. Two of the locomotives have the disc codes set for Exeter Central – one disc placed mid lower and the other up right this code was rigorously applied.

H.M.R.S ABJ830

No.35014 *Nederland Line* has arrived on the ash pit at Exmouth Junction after working the down Atlantic Coast Express to Exeter Central on 22 August 1950. The locomotive is in malachite green and carrying a BR number. The BR emblem was never applied to a malachite green Merchant Navy. This embellishment had to await blue livery. The tender in this view is unlettered.   The hole in the ACE headboard under the N in Atlantic enabled the electric headlamp to shine through.

A.E.West

S15 4-6-0 No.30847 awaits attention on the ash pit at Exmouth Junction at 2.40pm on 22 August 1950. 30847 has arrived tender first from either the main line or the marshalling yard, and after coaling and fire cleaning etc will continue beyond the coaler to the turntable. After turning it will run back and reverse into the loco yard facing up.

A.E.West

No. 35019 *French Line CGT* uses the 70ft turntable at Exmouth Junction on 22 August 1950.

A.E.West

No. 34048 *Crediton* in faded Malachite Green livery stands outside Exmouth Junction shed on 22 August 1950. The shed comprised of 12 roads each of which was 270ft long with pits running the length of the building. The high roof above the locomotive housed the lifting shop which was an extra section containing an overhead crane with a lifting capacity of 63 tons.

A.E.West

Exmouth Junction marshalling yard is on the left as No.31849 working an Ilfracombe line freight train drifts down the bank to Blackboy Tunnel and Exeter Central station on 18 September 1959. The locomotive will be on light steam with the Driver letting the wagons do the pushing, although with the possibility of adverse signals ahead at the busy Central station his hand will not be far from the vacuum brake.

A.E.West

The safety valves of No.34015 *Exmouth* lift at full pressure whilst awaiting departure from Exeter Central on 4 September 1964 with the Padstow portion of the last down weekday Atlantic Coast Express.

SOUTHERN-Images (www.southern-images.co.uk)

Right Top:
No. 34023 *Blackmoor Vale* arrives at Exeter Central on 4 May 1964 with the North Devon portion of the up Atlantic Coast Express. No.80041 stands alongside the down platform to the left.

Alec Swain/Transport Treasury

Right Bottom:
With a whisper of steam from the safety valves No.30451 *Sir Lamorak* has arrived at Exeter Central from Exmouth Junction on 4 September 1958 and stands in readiness alongside the up platform to work a passenger train to Salisbury. No.30451 has by now lost its Drummond watercart tender in favour of a Urie pattern one, which came from 32333 *Remembrance* in February 1957.

A.E.West

Having completed their tour of the Exmouth line, members of the S.C.T.S. South Western Limited rail tour, swan around the platform at Exeter Central before departing for Salisbury from No. 4 bay platform on 2 September 1962 hauled by No. 30861 *Lord Anson*.

Alec Swain/Transport Treasury

Having just emerged from the 184 yard long St. David's Tunnel with steam sanding gear turned on just in case of a wheel slip, and safety valves lifting No. 34021 *Dartmoor* tackles the final part of the ascent from Exeter St. Davids to Exeter Central on 22 July 1958.

R.C.Riley/Transport Treasury

Class Z 0-8-0T No.30955 stands in the goods yard at Exeter Central in August 1962. Eight members of this class were built at Brighton in 1929 and were the last heavy-duty steam shunting locomotives built by the Southern Railway.

Prorail UK (Durrant)/Transport Treasury

M7 0-4-4T No.374 in Southern Railway livery couples up to a L.N.E.R. CCT at Exeter Central on 25 June 1948. Exmouth Junction had a large stud of M7s, which were utilised on shunting and banking duties, plus working on the Exmouth/Sidmouth/Seaton/Budleigh/Bude branch lines.

Prorail UK (Durrant)/Transport Treasury

Steam swirls around Battle of Britain Class No.34062 *17 Squadron* working an up stopper at Exeter Central on 23 August 1963. The train stock comprises a GWR Fruit D and three coach set No.890.

A.E.West

No. 21C103 *Plymouth* is on the descent to Exeter St. Davids with the Plymouth portion of the Devon Belle on 7 September 1947. The steep angle of the descent can be gauged by the carriages standing on almost level ground to the right. *R.C.Riley/Transport Treasury*

2-6-0 No.31833 and another unidentified 2-6-0 tackle the 1 in 37 ascent from Exeter St. Davids Station towards Exeter Central with a passenger train from the Ilfracombe line on 20 August 1949.

M.Whitehouse Collection